PRINCE NEPTUNE

PRINCE NEPTUNE

Poetry and Prose

CODY R. SIMPSON

I am weighed on by an immense, burning desire for
something that I know exists but have not yet found.

For Rimbaud
For Baudelaire
For Kerouac
For Ginsberg
For Whitman
For Thoreau
For Dylan
For Morrison
For Atticus
For Poindexter
For my father

In this hour before dawn kitchen lights in houses speckled around the harbor are starting to twinkle like stars. Boats sway softly anchored undulating in the currents beneath the death black silk cloak of the sea while the soft bed of morning slowly rises like dough in the heat of the new Australian sun. The jeweled dawn passes in ephemeral fashion and big famous God in the sky only paints with his big famous colors for a moment before his boredom sets in and he washes the canvas blue until he feels like becoming an artist again.

Is language but a means of avoiding
silence and one's own solitude?
Or are we obligated as humans to use words
in an attempt to articulate silence?

The poetry lies not in the words but in
the silence between the words.

"Good waves at the bottom of Big Sur," I told him, my wise shaggy-haired Buddha-natured pops, "and there are cheap cabin motels in the woods that we could rent for a couple nights."

"Son yes yes yes! Let's go let's go! Go see and feel and witness the enormity of everything and the significance of everything! We give life meaning by living! We should get out there and just go. No use sittin' around!" he proclaimed, in a vehement burst of zest and desire to experience all that is good and fine on this eternal rotating earth.

PRINCE NEPTUNE

A thought is a ripple on the vast ocean of consciousness

PRINCE NEPTUNE

most days the monotony of society bores me to shit
tomorrow I shall take off my jacket and dance

with the next
hundred thousand
bombs
& wars
& years
the mountains
& trees
will sit in silence
primordial wisdom
& patience
waiting for us
to stop our fussing
& wake up for sunrises again

PRINCE NEPTUNE

i grew up barefoot
on the shores
mind reflection of feet
balanced
uninhibited
free from constraint

only as we grow up
we are told
to leave behind
our crystal island
of the mind
slip into the slipstream
of conformity
shirts
shoes
coffins for the sole
soul
un-learn freedom
& become
the caged man

as your television
sits upon its throne
inside
your president will tell you
it's okay
to burn the forest down
it's for the country

"the sky will part and the sun door will open once more
and we will pass back from time space into
the grand severed realm, perpetual"

two prophets in a bar discussing eternity
all the eternities
myriad eternities
innumerable

PRINCE NEPTUNE

"Sitting in coffee shop sunglasses on hungover talking
with women and reading and then all of a sudden
the sun comes out and washes a fabulous ray of light
directly over my small wooden table I'm slouched at
and I realize somewhere somebody out there knows."

Everybody's waiting
For the moment to arrive
I will clear my vision
See the water on the rise
The wave is nascent, beginning
Will we make it out alive?
Feet are stuck in quicksand
& we're running out of time

Point your guns at people
Pointing theirs down at the ground
There is no revelation
Without the silence of the sound
All your meditations
Like a diver heading down
Down into the kingdom
Where nobody wears the crown

Some mornings it's like the sun rises only for her

to discover
purity
subtle
almost atrophied
lying deep within all
clouded in the realm
of dualism

life
i am but tearing away layers
to find roots
melting away superfluities
and preserving only
quintessences

digging beneath the skin
to touch the crystal skeleton
in bone-white light illumination

a man at his root
is concerned
with none
but purity

PRINCE NEPTUNE

There are kings
who have died
failing to court her

O Apollo
With your ancient lyre & golden hair
A river of sound carves through the air
Shed your light upon the town & all the people there
Apollo

O Apollo
Twenty-three years I have sung for you
Evoking the vision to appear anew
In a forest of lies I abide by truth
Apollo

O Apollo
Grant me life & grant me reason
A change of heart and a change in season
Disaster to master the art of treason
Apollo

O Apollo
A glorious light in the depths of night
The children all have taken flight
Free from the shackles of malice & spite
Apollo

O Apollo
You've done for us what Christ could not

there's a big machine in the sky
a kind of electric lion with wings
coming straight at us

let me tell you about freedom
it cowers and shivers
as young women dance
in dark corners
to provoke your belt

suddenly
amidst lustful salutations
your eyes see the angel
with nothing but the senses to guide you
new life becomes as inevitable
as the milky coming of dawn

stone towers arise
erect in her night sky
warm and wet with rain
and as your thousand spirits soar
life explodes like roman candles
and she welcomes you
through the iron gates
to be born again

She could breathe peace into hostile earths

The incandescent experience of awakening to
oneself in the morning, eyes stinging, wondering
where you've just been all this time!

Ah! The universe! The bright and vibrant universe I've
been unaware of all throughout this long blind night!
Here in the universe! Where realities and dreamscapes
blend together like myriad colors on a canvas!

As dusk approaches it is time to rest once more, but my
mind is all at once concerned with where the original
stroke of paint lies, deep within this grand artwork!

mumbling down the streets of new york i hear jazz
echoing up from manholes in the ground
subway musicians hoofing their daily brass ecstasies
and all is cool and calm and fine
like always

PRINCE NEPTUNE

topping off the fuel
filled with azure cool
to the crystal pool

the silver engine hums

pirate's ship is done
a million ways to run

life for most is functional but uncreative

creativity in your everyday man is atrophied
due to the banality of his existence & his
concern for money, sex, & drink

gluttony is america
america is money
money is sex
sex is drink
drink is hedonism
hedonism is america

Artists are those most apt to seduce us to life

Sunken islands
Immersed in water
Teach your gentle ways

Electric eyes
Deliver me
From drowning in my cave

I, here, a mortal
Journey more into each passing moment
Waiting patiently
For my angel to return from the great wide heavens

Unlike the water in the deepest ocean
Or Picasso in 1902
Unlike the color of a sky so open
Me, I'm no longer blue

The tranquil hue of a turquoise gemstone
The talisman of shamans and kings
Ain't worth the treasure you bring me on your own
Nothing else means a thing

Some people dance by dangerous seaside
Some just can't hold through
But the Old Guitarist now holds his head high
All 'cause I have you
Me, I'm no longer blue

All my life I've possessed an overwhelming sense
of my own mortality, therefore an immense
desire to be free and to be free right now

She is a pure drop of water in an oil-ridden sea

PRINCE NEPTUNE

i dig the whole world at once
going infinitely inward and outward
all at once every day

dig the sky
dig the people
dig the music
dig the beer
dig it all

i dig the guru
he's the end and the beginning man
lets it all out
goes every direction
knows no time
never hung up
puts himself where he wants to be
but got nowhere to be
go like him and you'll get it!
yes!

PRINCE NEPTUNE

Man may only have a chance should he break through
all illusion and begin again in the wilderness

i drift and dance across wide azure
seascapes in search of everything
an attempt to merge back into nature once and for all
i am here to wrap gnarled reality around
my fingertips and clench my fists
i am here to do the damned thing for real this time

PRINCE NEPTUNE

an entire generation of people searching
within screens for God
look up not down you scattered wild creatures!
witness the undulations of ultimate spectacular reality!
hear the birdsong
let your mind burn burn burn with all the
poetry and fire of a thousand summers!

i sit
long blonde wet salt hair
eyes sinking deep in reflection
sensorium deranged
in constant pursuit of the unknown

let us begin a new world
let us do it all
we are the fresh young burgeoning wave of everything

The solitary seed nestled patiently in the
ground awaiting the warm sun
is the seed that becomes the tree

PRINCE NEPTUNE

one night
on the beach
vibratory waves pulsing
lysergic
behind my eyes

i saw a woman
in the shallows
wading

denim cut-off jeans
no shirt
blue beads around her neck

next moment
pointed right at me
grinned wide
motioned me over

i got a hard-on
and swam

When the senses are rationally disordered,
the poem rises from the depths of the
subconscious like a shimmering pearl

PRINCE NEPTUNE

once upon a time in Hollywood
guitars
gardens
chandeliers
sex
streetlamps
music as immense mass seduction
copulations in the back rows of movie theaters
houses in the hills
swimming pools
fin-tailed Cadillacs
lime juice
coffee shops in alleyways
comely girls with nose freckles smiling at you
ah Hollywood

Cinema, by nature, lays rhythmic order upon
arrhythmic and disorderly reality.

Theater and, later, cinema were born from the fear of death and the worship of myth in great societies. Great cultures and civilizations are psychologically inclined toward the enactment of myth and fantasy in order to palliate symptoms of fear and deliver themselves from the tedium or apparent meaninglessness of existence. The actor, in modern culture, plays the role of shaman. If immensely talented, he can place himself anywhere in time or space. The performer assumes the role of medicine man, experiencing levels of consciousness unattainable to the majority of the tribe, allowing witnesses to live vicariously through him and project their otherwise forbidden fantasies upon him. The portrayal of myth on stage or screen is as vital to man as food, water, or sex. There are now more original scripts developed in a Hollywood season than were written in the entire golden age of Greek theatre.

o boy
that one
she's the doll of the west
short-cut jacket and cigarette
she drives something out of a '50s film

a dreamer
with champagne eyes
just passing through
and doing so in real style

in the ancient night she flies once more
back to her home in the stars
i try to chase her there but fall short
for i cannot breathe up that high
in the radiant heaven where she lingers
i can only admire her from below
humble starry-eyed poet with a desire for that which is

most beautiful
& she is
most beautiful

all other muses sleep in winter forests
she is the one who swims in the sun & doesn't burn up

PRINCE NEPTUNE

A gentleman crouches beside a young boy drawing
waves on the pavement, 100 years from now
"Son, if you can possibly begin to imagine, I'll
share with you my photographs of the earth"

stay loose
stay on the run
don't let you catch yourself

The theater and the cinema
Are appropriations of idealized reality
The actor sees through impenetrable veils
The camera is the eye of God

I can transcend death
In strange astral sleep
Invigorating the senses
Visions come in droves to me
In my blue garden

I wish to be the quiet, undemonstrative artist
Making waves
And ways
For calmer days

I hear the West calling my name
Out there, the moon is a woman
A big illuminated diamond ball
With turquoise eyes
She sings to me
Neptune, Neptune
Come soon
And die in swift silence
Upon my shores
For I shall not wait forever
For my young men to undress

The sun became a tangerine
And painted for us skies of lavender
Then drowned slowly in the ocean
And the moon reclaimed her throne
in the sky once more

We rise
Tongues wagging, ecstatic
Dripping with warm life
Dreaming
Yet we revel in cool disguise

We design masks and sport them on balmy nights
To avoid conversation
To achieve sublimation
Then recede back into our caves
Of comfortable isolation

When will the all become the one?
When will we hear the great sound?

Enter now the eternal summer
The crystal tropics await
A tribe of deep electric jungle
Face paint
Drum rhythms
Semen sprawled upon trees
Marble palaces on canals
Naked women on great green lawns

Joyous, sensuous copulations
At night
Beneath the incoming rain

There may come a time we attend "nature theaters" to revive our experience of earthly sensation, showcasing scenery—oceans, forests, et cetera, of ages past. They may provide clean oxygenated air and simulate feelings of rain/sunlight on skin. A kind of four-dimensional cinematic sensory experience as a reminder of our "primitive" harmonious beginnings—to deliver us from our morbid concrete automobile world. A cinema of atavism. Environmentalists dread this concept.

PRINCE NEPTUNE

It was but a night
Now I've been bedridden for days
She gave me my entire life in an evening

"Let's go somewhere, find some drink and some
women—don't have to be wild, just somewhere
cool where we can go and dig everything!" he
said, as he looked at me with the cool strange
radiance that blue eyes always emit in daylight.

"I'm sober now mate can't you see that I'm here
trying to practice my meditations and do my
reading and get along fine without any uppers
or downers or whatever? Just leave me at peace
to practice my newfound asceticism. I miss my
girl and I want to be clear-minded for her!"

"Whew alright boy but I'm off to San Francisco!
Ocean Beach! Winding cliffside roads—all the way
up! And ya know what's at the end of them roads
boy? The dolls of the west man with eyes and smiles
like you've never seen in your life. And don't you
know it's alright to get high and run around mad
and intoxicated with the wild exuberance of a man
ready and willing to thrive in his own mortality?!"

He let out a final joyous screech and was off
in his car before I had the chance to open my
mouth. Boy was I jealous of fellas like that.

PRINCE NEPTUNE

Beware the tree uncarved by young lovers
Behold the unsailed and uncharted seas
To arrive by dusk and linger till morning
So witness the glory dawn yearns to achieve

I contend that I, a man no greater than he,
Am a programmed receiver of sensory glee
For the ancient white curtain of cloud on the sky
And the silk azure rippling of waves on the sea

Here we all stand with our smiles and our tears
The cool flow of all drift slowly across the years
Silver lining unwoven from the fabric of lives
The gentleman dies while the poem survives

We may wear different clothes, but
we wear the same sun

Freedom

I've been thinking of freedom
I've been thinking
Our holy rulers
Can go fuck themselves
Behind their unholy desks
With their unholy wars
Can go fuck themselves
With their big nuclear missiles

I've been thinking
Of complete withdrawal as protest
Asceticism as protest
Dignified rebellion

The messenger with the unwelcome message
Is likely to be shot
& man I've been thinking
Of freedom
I've been thinking
Of my heroes and their FBI files
This is why I write

Poesy
I write
To name the unnameable thing

Attempting to communicate
The original spark of life
But the motherfuckers would probably rather
Turn on the news
While I'm here thinking
Of freedom

I've been thinking
Of freedom
But I'm no poet
I just feel
The earth breathing
That's all

~

rolls of film capturing light reflections
celluloid
art-house films
copulations in black and white

drumming rhythms light the path
to alternate realms
the shaman sways in circular motion
as the conscious rational mind
becomes entranced by sound
& the profoundly rooted largely untamable
subconscious roams free

PRINCE NEPTUNE

psychic landscape
old beat-up car
acoustic guitar
white tee shirt
i haven't washed in weeks
on pacific coast highway
in monterey
carmel
frisco

slick trumpet players in bars
make me wanna
cut my hair

8mm camera
attempting to bring to life
words on a page
written in some bar
half-drunk
with brando and pocahontas
both on the mind

deep down
planted in the roots
of the soul
of a movie director
is the revolution seed

this here pirate plays the trumpet
and drinks from a brown paper bag
and smokes the kind of nature deemed forbidden
by human law
he collects songs in his head
and rambles in the dirt
this here pirate is mad and relishes in his madness
screech scram pow
running through the sacred streets at dawn
screaming
"abolish the war, revitalize the land,
cmon cmon cmon man do it"
my kind of pirate

reincarnation
the highest order prevails
even in disintegration

i urge you
to break through the boundaries of language
the steadfast iron gates of form
melting conception
melting perception
until all runs fluid
like water

i urge you
to see it only as it is

I am a walking hypocrisy because all life
is duality and the balance thereof

"I was up at 5 a.m. thinking about my life in Hollywood and all of the people I'd met and the sheer utter artificiality of it all that you can feel in your bones and under your skin no matter how many glasses of champagne they hand you or how many cameras they flash in your face trying to pin you up with some budding young starlet on your arm. I saw then in that moment that the only decent thing left to do was to go surfing."

Son, there are millions of fish in the sea
Find yourself a mermaid

"The glamour and surface sheen of it all masking its actual shallowness and possible emptiness and I took one more look around the party at everyone in their fabulous suits and gowns and figured I should dip out the back door immediately and take my car up through Malibu and beyond where I could really be alone."

Existential pirates
Traversing cosmic seas
Into the mystic
Under the black curtain of night
The stars drawing nigh
Their stories innumerable

The coast of Spain glistening in the distance
Misty and unaware
I sit on wooden bow
And think to myself in this moment
That old Wolfgang Amadeus Mozart
must have composed the universe

PRINCE NEPTUNE

running the vibrant streets at dusk
my fresh new woman and I
wine-soaked
finger-locked
in nothing but jeans
why should we sleep
let's fuck
we're here right now aren't we
you and I
in the universe

PRINCE NEPTUNE

life offers only one pursuit
ecstasy of the mind
all life and all action are in subconscious pursuit
of this and only this

The herald of the Aquarius age
Will come to us as a writer of films

Your beauty betrays you
For you wish to be shrouded in the cloak of night
Hidden from your beloved
But even in this darkness
Your eyes glisten like sapphires

We are soon to overthrow the natural kingdom
Our earth gently perishes
Meridian flow disrupted
With the slow death
Of an ancient species
With the rising of the tide
We live as though melting ice
Will turn to wine
We are calling for the end
Singing for it in fact

I tell you this
Join us on our delicate raft
We shall begin anew
Against the current
We shall paddle
Toward the tropics
Through Capricorn
Through warming golden coasts
Toward our mild equator once more

PRINCE NEPTUNE

warm women
rich girls
wet evenings
lysergic acid
leather
sex games
blonde hair
brilliance

PRINCE NEPTUNE

Give the eternal skeletons a rest
From the holy eye

The camera
Giving form to all facets of reality
Granting us sight of the diamond
Embedded in the rock
Of the earth

Sex is life's singular divine mechanism

I sing with the kings
And dance with the junkies
It all leads me to it

The closer we feel to death
The closer we are to life
Surfing monstrous waves
Riding motorcycles
Suffocation for the sake of orgasm

Let us rewrite the myths
Let us conceive of new religions
I have given my life to the golden eternity
Given my life to write the scriptures
To grant myself true life in the few good moments
Of ephemeral existence
And to send a shit-eating grin
Up to the gods
Through the green palms
On a sidewalk in California

Crystal dream
Cali queen
Radiant hand
Vibrant sand
I'm shot
It's a golden thing she's got

A thousand thrills
A thousand chills
Smoky eye
Pearly white
I'm hot
It's a golden thing she's got

I sang softly to her
In the last daylight
With a chorus of birds
In the heights of night
O if we could be heard
For whatever it's worth
By the rulers in the sky
They'd cry

L.A. is a field of diamonds
The night has a thousand eyes
I dance in the hills
Eager for everything

My mind is a crystal island
I relinquish control
And dance in the sand
Eager for everything

The camera is voyeur
I frame
Compose
And shoot life in the mainline vein direct
Eager for everything

Stars in silver rain
Chandelier treetops
I dance freely beneath
Eager for everything

I can transcend the earth
I can leave whenever I like
And return with visions
of Kings above
And still I am drawn back
To ocean
To cock
To city
To my worldly delights
Eager for everything

embarking on keen pursuit of truth
you must look into the mystic face of life itself
and in the cobalt dawn
you must go
and go
and go

leaving behind parents
teachers
friends
mentors

you must take life for yourself
you must write the books
you must compose the songs
you must shoot the films
you must paint the pictures
you must take life
and make life
yours

o delicate young woman you
listen here and listen close
run into the balmy night
singing with boisterous delight
for someday you will lay to rest
beside your tired prince

you must first cultivate the senses
& then detach from them
take a breath to prepare for total immersion

Be gone with the organized world
Introduce sacred disorder
Deconstruct all form
All matter
Until it is once again dispersed
Into the four corners of the universe
Silent
Oscillating
Destroy all that man has created
Tombs
Scrolls
All evidence
For God too was an artist
Destroyed by his creations

Resurrect the old poetry of the earth
Introduce the shaman
Let him reach out
To grasp hold of the original conception of vision
Once more
And when he comes
Into the milky crotch
Of the cosmos
All will fall still
For the jungle may be dark
But it is full of diamonds

with a single stroke
a single strum
we ride
upon the Zuvuya

all is clear
empty
self-illuminating
third plane
karma unfolding
just beyond the horizon
to a path of many windings
it is here that winged thoughts pour forth
into words

we faked love for about an hour
and in the cool cool night i left
silent and hazy and full of wine

The further out you venture, the more infinitely
vast and complex you find the space to be.
The deeper you dive, the further
you find the floor to fall.
I think this is true of the internal human mind
and of objective reality and the world.

I hope to coalesce all of my electric fragments
And become a whole man one day

at the helm of the ship of eternity
we ramble in phosphorescent ecstasy
beaming at the sight of everything

Tranquil Vision

The monstrous wildfire luminescent trees
are ablaze in Southern California
While the Santa Ana winds blow smog back in the faces
of us naive robotic automobile-driving polluters

I sit in strange afternoon denim jeans blue beaded
necklace roped around my neck silent in meditation
witnessing solitary observational thought
Calm quiet essence of the original
human mind persevering beneath the
ruins of this eternal time temple

Emit your holy or unholy projections
upon me and I will embrace them
Project your desires upon me and
I will fulfill them for you
I will take the trip
I will dance in the hills under the shimmering
sun, bronzed and ecstatic as others watch up
with open jaws in village street below

I will stand on the precipice of towering
cliffside without fear, leap into midair without
hesitation, and plunge into the depths
on my own and always on my own

O vision, tranquil vision
Vision vision vision
Take me here, now, in the open
Warm vision
Eternal vision
Take me here, now, in the open
I know of the superfluities that mask your pure cool face
Vision vision vision
Tranquil vision
I know you're in there
I know you
Let me see you
Let me inside of you
No more games
Let me see you
I lust for you
Take off your clothes
For I must see you now
I must

Only in this world of earthly desire does
the eternal vision engage in foreplay

~

she does not dance with the angels
she dances with the man she loves
to the song she hears in her head
when she sees him

the closer you are to the elements
the closer to the source
the closer to authentic and original matter
the more spirit-oriented you become

nature breeds instinct
surround yourself with original matter whenever
possible

swim in ocean
hold stones
touch trees
walk on sand
you will feel better

My visions are easy and free-flowing. The conflict and difficulty arise during the process of translation of vision into form. The intangible into the tangible. The metaphysical into the physical. The visions must be able to be read, sensed, heard, or felt in an inclusive, comprehensive, and understandable manner in order to be widely appreciated. Every being on earth has access to vision. The challenge comes in bringing it into form.

PRINCE NEPTUNE

i intend to
drift into
my subconscious
like a bird in flight
calmly unaware
of the task at hand
the journey
from womb to tomb
as subtle as
the passing wind
dear god
just don't let me die
on a motorcycle
or drown
beneath the
pulsing swells
i wish myself well
to fade peacefully
at one hundred and eight
with a sense of humor
and a mind drained dry

PRINCE NEPTUNE

In the wake of witnessing totality
Just before the coming of dawn
A newborn sun evokes childlike ecstasy
And a fresh zest for reimmersion into the trip

Wade your way into this uncivilized island
This untraversed territory
We are the eclipse of the Sunset Strip

I know how it feels
To have wings on my heels
And the sun on my shoulders
In the foreign depths of summer
Flying gracefully with silver belt and golden locks

Death to my former self
An ascension to heaven
To the cinematic skies
And to the black silk sheet of night riddled with stars
Like TV static

can humanity's segregated fragments be coalesced
through some kind of primitive ritual? destructing
bourgeois consciousness and resurrecting a
unified electricity between all things? will it
require the unwavering movement of a single
man or the involvement of the entire tribe?

Don't fall for her flowers, but for her roots

believe in the crowd
or believe in the great sound
your choice

my soul is wrapped up in a fast car with a coast
to reach and a woman at the end of the road

PRINCE NEPTUNE

I call upon my brothers to comprehend
the rapid unwinding of daybreak
the omnipresence of truth
I'm called back once and for all in
order to seek some meaning
some obligation
I'm sent into the desert to uncover the ancient tales
and to build the raft for my friends
on which we can cross the river of uncertainty
and enter the realm
in which truth and tale
are one in the same

observe most carefully
for the summer martyr
is crafting
a fresh river of sound
that winds and carves
through thin air
like a sword

PRINCE NEPTUNE

we must create new calendars
new measurements of time and space
let us invent new words and phrases
let us craft a universal language that all can decipher
let us reinvigorate and refresh all
modes of communication
conjuring a style so modern and so radiant that men
and women will travel from distant lands to hear it

PRINCE NEPTUNE

"And I heard the sound of water through the windows of
an old small fish shack as I ate my lunch beside broken
rusty ice cream coolers, crabs, wooden tables and
chairs, glass bottles, overgrown plants atop counters,
pictures of fishermen from decades past yellowing
with antiquity on the splintered walls while acoustic
guitar-playing kids sit out on the sidewalk and young
women in berets with short hair grin with cigarettes
pursed in rosy lips and there are old alleyways down
the street behind the village theater with drunkards
slouched and gray and drunk who know the true life
secret that everyone's always searching for but would
never think of going behind the village theater to ask
the drunkards so we're stuck forever anyway. Man."

you are far off
on some foreign coast
in a white gown
made of silk
and I'm here
half-dead
and hungover
listening to jazz

PRINCE NEPTUNE

Man has never discovered new islands
in previously charted waters

To fix a broken system, one must first
break the self the system has fixed

malibu burns

the sea is alight with a thousand fires
the heart is alive with a thousand suns
the soul may only extinguish
what the eye cannot see
and the sea we see
is the sea that burns

the sea alight with a thousand fires
and the heart alive with a thousand suns

~

here on this day
we journey further into the illusion
adrift in the great dream
yearning for entry into the severed realm

I flew toward the open sky
With Apollonian knowledge and righteousness of mind
Playing my six strings like they
were the strings of heaven
And they were the strings of heaven
I sang for townsfolk of many origins
Like Apollo atop mythical Greek Olympus
I vowed to shed the light of the sun upon all I greeted

The lone wolf performs solitary salutations in an attempt at transcendence and in search of new visions. If he can collect that which he seeks he is obligated to descend and present his findings to the rest of the tribe. He is the dazed, recalcitrant, rebel prince dancing in the hills above the town while everyone watches from the ground in astonishment. "Look! Look at him!"

there's no terror in riding the wave
only in the anticipation of getting up

When the fame and the flesh cease
to fulfill my earthly desires
I will shed my skin and venture inward
In search of greater glories

In my mind I can move mountains

PRINCE NEPTUNE

cool sensations

i have felt the cool sensations
salt on skin
skin crisp from sunrays
off to the next wild destination
in search of the next golden adventure

i've sat by bonfires at dusk
under bloodred skies
mosquitoes
guitars
congas
women in white sarongs
discussing eternity with those who know eternity
and i have felt
my sunburnt back on airplane seats
my feet ripped with reef scars
my voice hoarse from ecstatic chanting
with my friends
my people
who know eternity

it's hard to speak with those
chasing the next illusory reward
the next great dollar
in big cities
in ties
in limousines
in banks
in office chairs

those who disregard
vibration

but i know one day
everyone will know eternity
he will know eternity
she will know eternity
they will know eternity
and i will know eternity

i can see the blue prisms suspended
in midair chandelier summer
i can see the central sun
dancing in the vast sky
and i will know eternity

contemporary currents surpass me
i am trapped within my own realm
but my realm exists in eternity
i must live
according to broader laws
the ground must crumble
beneath crowds
temples of the ages
must fall to ashes
in the face of eternity
the eternity that i will know

o man
such a young death

for a boy king
but he will know eternity

i am tired
of undisciplined consciousness
i wish to catch the essence of everything
far removed
from it all
and i wish to know eternity

o man
such a young death
for a boy king
but he will know eternity

the boulevardiers
will never see
poetry in motion
or the gleaming rewards
that lie
just beyond the pit of discomfort
but that'll be my secret

ok
signing out
farewell Australia
keep our world warm for us
i am barefoot in the airport now
off to know eternity

~

I am interested in the inexhaustible reservoir of energy.
I am interested in the illuminations that craft the alive
electric emptiness that brings us closer to all-knowing.

PRINCE NEPTUNE

New illuminations
Aquatic scintillations
Dogs roaming in wet azure gardens
Songs foaming from dazed disorderly mind
As I drink the wine
And drown myself
I arrive suddenly
At the unknown
A prince of breathtaking measures
Complete with trident and treasures

PRINCE NEPTUNE

notes on vision
~the new moon in tropical capricorn
~study of energy/water interactions
~abhorrence of aristocratic behavior/snobbishness
~class selectiveness and preferential social treatment
~aristocracy = hereditary/not achieved of the human spirit
~rebellion against social hierarchies
~Australian though also son of entire earth
~destruction of borders/abolishment of nationalism
~ill-adapted to modern society and horrified at idea of
occupying any institutionalized position within it
~young people of the ocean grove no longer sleep in coffins
~attempts to assign sacred characters to historical
phenomena carry no conviction with me
~theatrical approach to existence, balletic and fluid
~the "now" requires undivided attention
~internal battle between urge to retract and pursue
strictly metaphysical expansion and transcendence or
to immerse myself into reality and pursue endeavors/
ambitions; stand on front lines of social battles
~deep sense of paradise lost
~looking forward and greatly anticipating
some kind of apocalypse within the general
bourgeois conventionalism of society
~orthodoxy denotes the organized collective
wielding power over the free personality of man
~but I guess I can thank God for a few free waves

~

116

by Cody R. Simpson

Andrews McMeel Publishing
a division of Andrews McMeel Universal
1130 Walnut Street, Kansas City, Missouri 64106

www.andrewsmcmeel.com

20 21 22 23 24 BVG 10 9 8 7 6 5 4 3 2 1
ISBN: 978-1-5248-5399-0
Library of Congress Control Number: 2019956457

Editor: Patty Rice
Art Director: Diane Marsh
Production Editor: Meg Daniels
Production Manager: Carol Coe
Illustration © Getty Images, pop_jop

ATTENTION: SCHOOLS AND BUSINESSES
Andrews McMeel books are available at quantity discounts
with bulk purchase for educational, business, or sales
promotional use. For information, please e-mail the Andrews
McMeel Publishing Special Sales Department:
specialsales@amuniversal.com.